presents

by Vicky Jones

The One had its world premiere on 26th February 2014
at Soho Theatre, London

CAST

Phoebe Waller-Bridge	JO
Rufus Wright	HARRY
Lu Corfield	KERRY

CREATIVE TEAM

Vicky Jones	Writer
Steve Marmion	Director
Anthony Lamble	Designer
Ben Ormerod	Lighting Designer
Gareth Fry	Sound Designer
Nadine Rennie CDG	Casting Director
Sara Joyce	Assistant Director
Robert Holmes	Production Manager
Brett Yount	Fight Director
Caroline Meer	Deputy Stage Manager
Charlotte McBrearty	Stage Manager

CAST

PHOEBE WALLER-BRIDGE JO

Phoebe is a graduate of RADA. Theatre credits include: *Fleabag* (Underbelly/Soho; winner of The Stage Best Solo Performance 2013); *Mydidae* (Soho/Trafalgar Studios); *Hay Fever* (Noël Coward Theatre, West End); *Tribes* (Royal Court); *Rope* (Almeida); *2nd May 1997, Like A Fishbone* and *66 Books* (Bush); *Roaring Trade* (Soho); *Crazy Love* (Paines Plough). Television credits include: *Flack, The Revengers, Blandings, Scrotal Recall, Henry, Bad Education, London Irish, The Café, The Night Watch, How Not to Live Your Life*. Radio credits include: *Vincent Price and the Horror of the English Blood Beast, Burns and the Bankers* (Radio 4); *Money* (Radio 3). Film credits include: *Man Up, Albert Nobbs, The Iron Lady*. Phoebe is also an award-winning playwright (*Fleabag*) and co-Artistic Director of DryWrite.

RUFUS WRIGHT HARRY

Theatre credits include: *The Audience* (Gielgud); *Titanic* (MAC Belfast); *The 39 Steps* (Criterion); *The Empire* (Royal Court); *Serious Money* (Birmingham Rep); *Private Lives* (Hampstead); *Crown Matrimonial* (Guildford/tour); *Frost/Nixon* (Donmar Warehouse/Gielgud); *Mary Stuart* (Donmar Warehouse/Apollo); *Journey's End* (Playhouse/Duke of York's); *Hay Fever* (Basingstoke Haymarket); *The Madness of George III* (West Yorkshire Playhouse/Birmingham Rep); *Trust Byron, Life With an Idiot, Franziska* (Gate); *Single Spies* (West Yorkshire Playhouse); *The Secret Garden* (Salisbury Playhouse); *The Backroom* (Soho); *Richard II* (London Pleasance). Television credits include: *Foyle's War, Little Crackers, EastEnders, New Tricks, Miranda, White Van Man, Five Daughters, The Thick of It, Taking the Flak, The Bill, Fanny Hill, Doctors, Extras, The Quatermass Experiment, P.O.W, The Secret, Bomber, Boyz Unlimited*. Film credits include: *The Special Relationship, Quantum of Solace, Spy Game* and the forthcoming *The Face of an Angel*. Radio credits include: over twenty radio plays for BBC Radio, including three series of *North by Northamptonshire*.

LU CORFIELD KERRY

Trained at RADA. Theatre credits include: *The Big Idea: Sex – Friday Night Sex* (Royal Court); *Medea* (Headlong Theatre); *Days of Significance* (Royal Shakespeare Company); *Such Tweet Sorrow* (RSC on Twitter); *The Girlfriend Experience* (Young Vic/Plymouth Drum/Royal Court); *Sports Day* (Arcola/The Miniaturists); *Danny the Champion of the World* (Birmingham Stage Company); *Really Living* (Brighton Ourstory Productions); *The Ghost Sonata* (Goat and Monkey); *The Shoemakers Holiday* (Rose) and *The Veronika Sessions* (The Hobbs Factory/Arcola). Television includes *Doctors* (series regular), *Game of Thrones, The Johnny and Inel Show, The Dumping Ground, Stella, Quick Cuts, Casualty, Watson and Oliver, Rev, Random, Threesome, Quiff and Boot, Candy Cabs, EastEnders, Girl Friday, The Bill, Consuming Passion, Holby City, The Golden Hour* and *Nighty Night.* Film includes *The Woman in Black* and *The Isle of Spagg.*

CREATIVE TEAM

VICKY JONES WRITER

Vicky is co-Founder and co-Artistic Director of DryWrite, Associate Company at Soho Theatre. With DryWrite, she has commissioned and directed many short plays from some of the country's leading new writing talent. The company have performed shows at theatres including Hampstead Theatre, York Theatre Royal, Liverpool Everyman, Trafalgar Studios and The Roundhouse, where DryWrite originally commissioned and directed Simon Stephens's monologue *T5*. She directed Phoebe Waller-Bridge's hit solo show, *Fleabag* for the Edinburgh Festival 2013 and a subsequent run at the Soho Theatre. She also directed premiere productions of Jack Thorne's *Mydidae* at Soho and then Trafalgar Studios, and James Graham's *The Tour Guide*, a hit of the 2011 Edinburgh Festival. She has assisted at the National, the Royal Court, in the West End and off-Broadway. Vicky trained as a director on the Royal Court/Channel 4 Young Directors Scheme, the Gate Theatre Trainee Directors Scheme and the National Theatre Studio Directors course. This is Vicky's first play.

STEVE MARMION DIRECTOR

Steve is Artistic Director of Soho Theatre. For Soho Theatre, Steve has directed *The Night Before Christmas*, *Pastoral*, the French and English productions of *Address Unknown*, *Realism* (Whatsonstage Award-nominated), *Mongrel Island*, *Fit and Proper People*, *Utopia* and *The Boy Who Fell Into a Book*. Prior to joining the company in 2010, Steve directed *Macbeth* for Regent's Park Open Air Theatre and *Dick Whittington*, *Jack and the Beanstalk* and *Aladdin* for the Lyric Hammersmith. In 2009 he directed the highly successful production of *Edward Gant's Amazing Feats of Loneliness* for Headlong Theatre which received rave reviews on tour and at Soho Theatre. In 2008 he had three critically praised successes with *Vincent River* in New York, *Only the Brave* in Edinburgh and *Metropolis* in Bath. He also transferred Rupert Goold's *Macbeth* onto Broadway. Steve was assistant, then Associate Director, at the

RSC over two years from 2006–07. In 2004 he directed several premieres for Sir Alan Ayckbourn at the Stephen Joseph Theatre and returned to direct the Christmas show in 2006. He has worked with the National Theatre, RSC, in the West End, on Broadway, at the Royal Court, Lyric Hammersmith, Theatre Royal Plymouth, Theatre Royal Bath, Watford Palace Theatre, Sherman Theatre Cardiff and Edinburgh Festival. *Only the Brave* (2008) was nominated for Best New Musical and Best New Music and his production of *Madam Butterfly's Child* (2004) and *Mad Margaret's Revenge* (2005) won the London One Act Theatre Festival.

ANTHONY LAMBLE DESIGNER

Anthony's theatre credits include *Shush, The Passing, The East Pier, Bookworms, The Comedy of Errors* and *The Playboy of the Western World* (Abbey); *Ciara* (Traverse/Glasgow Citizens); *The Artist Man and The Mother Woman, The Arthur Conan Doyle Appreciation Society* (Traverse); *The Two Worlds of Charlie F* (Theatre Royal Haymarket/Pleasance Edinburgh); *For Once* (Pentabus); *Relatively Speaking* (Watermill); *Shivered* (Southwark); *The Complaint, Everything is Illuminated* (Hampstead); *The Price* (West End/Tricycle/tour); *The Caucasian Chalk Circle, Translations, Sing Yer Heart Out for the Lads, A Midsummer Night's Dream, As You Like It* (National Theatre); *Measure for Measure, Richard III, The Roman Actor, King Baby* (Royal Shakespeare Company); *The Entertainer* (Old Vic) as well as numerous productions for the Royal Court, Menier Chocolate Factory, West Yorkshire Playhouse and the Bush Theatre. Dance and Opera credits include *Facing Viv* (English National Ballet), *L'Orfeo* (Japan tour), *Palace in the Sky* (English National Opera) and *Broken Fiction* (Royal Opera House).

BEN ORMEROD LIGHTING DESIGNER

Ben's previous productions for Soho Theatre include *Fit and Proper People* and *A Night at the Dogs*. Other theatre credits include Spanish Golden Age (Theatre Royal Bath/Ustinov Season); *The Colleen Bawn* (Druid); *The Beauty Queen of Leenane* (Druid/West End/Broadway/Sydney/ Toronto); *The Heresy of Love, Macbeth, The Revenger's Tragedy, Henry V, Julius Caesar* (RSC); *King Lear* (Glasgow Citizens); *Onassis, Macbeth, Legal Fictions* (West End); *Zorro!* (West End/UK tour/US/Japan); *Welsh Boy, Deadkidssongs, The Double, The Phoenix of Madrid, Iphigenia* (Bath); *Dimetos* (Donmar Warehouse); *Two Men of Florence* (Boston); *The Crucible* (Lyric Belfast); *Translations, Last Days of the Reluctant Tyrant* (Abbey, Dublin); *The Changeling, Hedda Gabler, The Doll's House* (ETT); *Bent, Uncle Vanya, The Winter's Tale, In Remembrance of Things Past* (National Theatre) and numerous productions for Propeller including *The Comedy of Errors* and *A Midsummer Night's Dream*. Recent opera and dance credits include *Der Ring des Nibelungen* (Longborough Festival Opera); *Les Noces* (Grand Théâtre Geneva) and *See Blue Through* for Phoenix Dance Company.

GARETH FRY SOUND DESIGNER

Gareth trained at the Central School of Speech and Drama in theatre design. Recent work includes: *Let the Right One In* (NT Scotland, Royal Court and Dundee); *A CBeebies Christmas Carol* (CBeebies); *The Noise* (Unlimited); *The Secret Agent* (Theatre O, Traverse and Young Vic); *David Bowie Is* (V&A); *Shun-kin* (Complicite, NY, LA, Japan, Singapore); *Black Watch* (NT Scotland/US tour); *Othello* (National Theatre); *Hamlet* (RSC); *Reise Durch die Nacht* (Schauspiel, Cologne, Avignon Festival and Theatre Treffern, Berlin); *Trojan Women* (Gate), *Longing* (Hampstead); *Fräulein Julie* (Schabühne, Berlin and Barbican, London); Soundscape Design for the Opening Ceremony of the Olympic Games, *The Master and Margarita* (Complicité). Awards include: Laurence Olivier Award 2007 for *Waves*; Helpmann Award 2008 and Olivier Award 2009 for *Black Watch*; IRNE Award 2012 for *Wild Swans* in Boston.

SARA JOYCE ASSISTANT DIRECTOR

Sara studied Drama at Trinity College, Dublin, before training at the Ecole Jacques Lecoq in Paris. She was most recently Assistant Director to Steve Marmion on *The Night Before Christmas* by Anthony Neilson, at Soho Theatre. Directing credits include *The Wonderful World of Disoccia* by Anthony Neilson, *Cloud 9* by Caryl Churchill and *Attempts On Her Life* by Martin Crimp. Sara is co-founder of Whispering Beasts, a new company which won the Deutsche Bank Award for Drama. Their debut project *The Playboy Variations* will play at the new Ophelia Theatre, Dalston, in spring 2014. Sara is also director of *Click*, a new play by Kate Kennedy, which will also run at the Ophelia Theatre in 2014.

London's most vibrant venue for new theatre, comedy and cabaret.

Soho Theatre is a major creator of new theatre, comedy and cabaret. Across our three different spaces we curate the finest live performance we can discover, develop and nurture. The company works with theatre makers and companies in a variety of ways, from full producing of new plays, to co-producing new work, working with associate artists and presenting the best new emerging theatre companies that we can find. We have numerous writers and theatre makers on attachment and under commission, six young writers and comedy groups and we read and see hundreds of shows a year – all in an effort to bring our audience work that amazes, moves and inspires.

'Soho Theatre was buzzing, and there were queues all over the building as audiences waited to go into one or other of the venue's spaces. [The audience] is so young, exuberant and clearly anticipating a good time.' *Guardian*

We attract over 170,000 audience members a year. We produced, co-produced or staged over forty new plays in the last twelve months. Our social enterprise business model means that we maximise value from Arts Council and philanthropic funding; we actually contribute more to government in tax and NI than we receive in public funding.

sohotheatre.com

Keep up to date:

sohotheatre.com/mailing-list
facebook.com/sohotheatre
twitter.com/sohotheatre
youtube.com/sohotheatre

Registered Charity No: 267234

Soho Theatre, 21 Dean Street, London W1D 3NE
sohotheatre.com
Admin 020 7287 5060 | Box Office 020 7478 0100

THANK YOU

We are immensely grateful to our fantastic Soho Theatre Friends and Supporters. Soho Theatre is supported by Arts Council England. This theatre has the support of the Channel 4 Playwrights' Scheme sponsored by Channel 4 Television.

We would also like to thank those supporters who wish to stay anonymous as well as all of our Soho Theatre Friends.

Production support: AKA and Nancy Poole PR. Cover image: Michael Windsor-Ungureanu.

THE ONE

Vicky Jones

For Phoebe Waller-Bridge

Acknowledgements

With thanks to:

Tobias Menzies, Sian Clifford, Phil Porter, Simon Stephens, Jack Thorne, Conor Woodman, Giles Smart, Andy Gout, Mark Shepherdson, Steve Marmion, Nina Steiger, Nadine Rennie, David Luff and all at the Soho Theatre, Francesca Moody, Caroline Meer, Sara Joyce, Rufus Wright, Lu Corfield, Charlotte McBrearty, Sarah Liisa and all at Nick Hern, and the Verity Bargate Award panel.

Special, massive thanks to Adam Brace.

The One was originally workshopped by DryWrite.

V.J.

Characters

JO, *twenty-nine*
HARRY, *thirty-nine*
KERRY, *thirty-six*

Key

A space in the text indicates how long the silences last.

/ indicates an overlap in speech.

The absence of a full stop at the end of a line means the thought is unfinished or interrupted. The next line can often follow on immediately or almost overlap.

ONE

The lounge. About 10 p.m. Saturday. HARRY *and* JO *are having sex whilst watching porn.*

JO *is sitting on top of him and also eating Wotsits.*

Both appear more interested in the porn than in each other.

JO *is alternately jerking up and down a bit, and nibbling on a Wotsit.*

JO *throws a Wotsit in the air and tries to catch it in her mouth.*

HARRY	Can you not?
JO	YES! [*Or* 'BOLLOCKS!' *if she doesn't catch it.*] What?
HARRY	With the Wotsits
JO	What with the Wotsits?
HARRY	It's minging.
JO	You want me to starve?
HARRY	You had dinner.
JO	Gone!

The sex becomes more rhythmic, more intense.

JO *resembles a jockey, deep in concentration.*

HARRY *is touching her body but she doesn't respond.*

JO *picks up the remote and turns off the porn.*

She begins channel surfing.

HARRY *appears neither surprised nor annoyed.*

She climbs off him and watches the TV.

HARRY	A week isn't going to kill us.
	She continues to surf.
	Can we at least talk about the possibility
JO	Ah, *The Boy Who Gave Birth to his Twin*?
HARRY	You've seen that one.
JO	Shock docs make me happy – don't you want to know what's going on in the world?
HARRY	Tell me what's going on in the world.
JO	A fetus can pitch its placenta on a little child's lower intestine.
HARRY	Why do I need to know that?
JO	It's enhanced our understanding of fetuses. And what better night to polish up on that specialist subject?
HARRY	Yes.
JO	Yes. So?
HARRY	So?
JO	So, watch it with me. And afterwards, there's a documentary for you, about the British Museum.
HARRY	D'you know I've never been to the British Museum.
JO	It was made for you.
HARRY	What's it like?
JO	British.
HARRY	You've never been either.
JO	Let's go some time.
HARRY	When?
JO	Let's go tomorrow.
HARRY	If we're not at the hospital.

JO   Sure.

          She continues to watch the TV.

HARRY   Would there be any point in asking you to turn
          that off?

JO   I'm gonna do my CV in a minute.

HARRY   Jo!

JO   Okay okay. Okay.

          JO *turns off the TV.*

          Okay.

HARRY   Now then.

JO   Now then.

HARRY   Wait – have they texted?

JO   Not

          JO *checks her phone.*

          No.

HARRY   Because three centimetres is not the same / as two
          centimetres.

JO   You said.

HARRY   So which is it?

JO   I don't know, it's not my vagina.

HARRY   Cervix. It's your sister's though, aren't you getting
          sympathy pangs?

JO   Two.

HARRY   Alright so it looks like we're in for the long haul.

JO   Hm strap in.

HARRY   Now then.

JO *has been studying her arm.*

JO	Did you ever notice these tiny white spots on my arm? They totally freak me out. I keep thinking I'm getting skin cancer or something
HARRY	You're not getting skin cancer
JO	It's a condition called. Well it has a name. The skin loses its pigment and if overexposed to sunlight the effect can be carcinogenic.
HARRY	I said keep off those websites
JO	Imagine being encased in the thing that's killing you. Skin's the biggest organ of the human body. Once you get it, it spreads at an uncontrollable rate.
HARRY	Your paranoia spreads at an uncontrollable rate.
JO	I might have stage three melanoma.
HARRY	You have no symptoms.
JO	(*Darkly.*) Exactly.

JO *begins to fiddle with the remote again.*

HARRY	I think a good grounding in statistics would really enhance your life.

JO *goes to turn the telly on again.* HARRY *takes the remote out of her hand and looks at her.*

Why don't we just try it, for a week?

JO	Do you think I'd make a good teacher?
HARRY	A thinking week
JO	Because I *am* very encouraging
HARRY	When we both *think* about what we want
JO	Well I'm starting to *think* I could really be a good teacher.
HARRY	I think you'd make a brilliant teacher but it's not what you want to do

JO   Maybe it is. Maybe I just haven't done it. Don't
                leave me.

HARRY   We're not leaving each other. That's not what I'm
                saying.

JO   It is.

HARRY   I'm saying there are certain things I can't

JO   I know

HARRY   Take, again

JO   I know

HARRY   And I need you to be sure.

JO   Ha! Rob told me the best chat-up line today, it's
                for boys so you have to do it to your students.

HARRY   I don't want to chat anyone up.

JO   Wait, wait, so a guy walks into a nightclub right and

HARRY   JO

JO   A GUY walks into a nightclub right and

HARRY   This is stupid

JO   And he says to a girl, 'excuse me,'

HARRY   Please stop it

JO   He says 'excuse me, but do you know if there's
                a vet in the house?' And the girl says 'no', like,
                'why?'

                JO *is bending both her arms with the hands
                facing outwards, pulling an arm flex, resembling
                two swans.*

                and he says
                'cos these swans are siiiickkkk'.
                Because they look like swans

HARRY   (*Mildly amused.*) Very good

JO   You can have that. In your week off. You can use
          that.

HARRY   I'm not sure I've got the swans for it.

JO   There's a girl outside.

HARRY   You want me to try it *now*?

JO   No I think you know her.

HARRY   Where?

          He looks out.

          It's Kerry

JO   I know it's Kerry

HARRY   How long's she been standing there?

JO   Couple of minutes.

HARRY   Why didn't you say so?

JO   Dunno

HARRY   Why didn't you say it was Kerry before?

JO   I wasn't sure it was Kerry before.

HARRY   Does she want to come in?

JO   Well she hasn't knocked so let's assume not.

HARRY   Shall I open the door?

JO   She hasn't knocked!

HARRY   No. But she's here.

JO   Yeah but she might change her mind

HARRY   What's she doing here? It's

          He looks at his watch.

JO   She's your friend.

HARRY   She's our friend.

JO   Let's just pretend we haven't seen her, she might
            go away.

HARRY   Right this is stupid.

            HARRY *goes to open the door.*

JO   Wait!

            HARRY *ignores her and goes to let her in.*

HARRY   (*Off.*) Kerry!

TWO

Less than a minute later. KERRY*,* JO *and* HARRY *are standing in the lounge.* KERRY *has clearly been crying.*

KERRY	I'm sorry to
HARRY	It's alright.
JO	It's alright.
KERRY	I'm sorry Jo, I thought
HARRY	It's alright.
KERRY	Is it alright?
HARRY	It is
JO	Is it?
KERRY	It's not is it?
HARRY	It is
JO	It completely is
KERRY	No, it's not, it's not alright, it's late you are obviously in the middle of. Something, I should definitely go.
HARRY	Really?
KERRY	Yeah, I should go.
	KERRY *starts to leave.*
HARRY	Hold on. Has something happened?
KERRY	I don't know why I came here, I just started walking, and this is where I ended up
JO	Bizarro
HARRY	Would you like a drink? Tea. Jo would you get Kerry a cup of tea?

JO	If she wants some tea / I can
HARRY	She'll want some tea
JO	She didn't say she wanted / tea
HARRY	But I bet she does want tea – Kerry would you like a cup of tea?
JO	She hasn't asked for tea
KERRY	I don't want to put you out
HARRY	She's being polite.
JO	She doesn't want to put us out
HARRY	Just go and make the tea, would you, baby?
JO	She didn't ask for tea.
KERRY	Actually, tea would be / great
JO	Great! Well there you go, turns out she does want tea. Harry you were right.
	Oh sorry, I was making the tea wasn't I?
	JO leaves.
HARRY	Sorry.
KERRY	I'm disturbing you.
HARRY	And sorry about Jo.
KERRY	Jo's Jo.
HARRY	Something like that.
KERRY	And are you still thinking about
HARRY	About what?

KERRY   That, week

HARRY   It's very

KERRY   Sure

HARRY   It's all very

KERRY   It's okay. It's okay.

           Did you get my um

HARRY   I've barely looked at it with

KERRY   Yeah. It's okay.

HARRY   You've been crying.

KERRY   Not really

HARRY   Why?

           Is it Bradley?

KERRY   I don't want to be dramatic.

HARRY   What's he done?

KERRY   Nothing. He.
           He didn't do anything. Exactly.

HARRY   Exactly?

           JO *calls through to the living room, slightly
           too loudly.*

JO   Milk and sugar Kerry?

KERRY   Yes please

HARRY   Look at me. Has he hurt you?

           If he's laid a finger on you

JO	Biscuit?
KERRY	Um
HARRY	Kerry?
JO	BISCUIT?
HARRY	Do you want a biscuit.
KERRY	Um. I
HARRY	Just bring them through darling
JO	What?
HARRY	Just bring the biscuits through.
JO	Righto.
HARRY	You don't have to talk about it now but if he's laid a finger on you
JO	One lump or two?
HARRY	Just bring everything through.
KERRY	Um, two please.
JO	CHOCOLATE / FINGER?
HARRY	Just bring *all* of the possible options you could possibly have with tea, through. Bring it all through.
KERRY	I want to talk about it. I just don't know where
HARRY	If he's laid the littlest finger on the littlest hair on your head
KERRY	Dude, of course he's laid a finger on me, he's laid all his fingers on me.
HARRY	Fine but
KERRY	He's laid everything everywhere
HARRY	But has he
JO	Kerry are you a Scorpio?

HARRY   Kerry. What's he done?

JO   You've got Scorpio written all over you

HARRY   Excuse me.

         HARRY leaves to the kitchen.

         The sound of a plate violently smashing. KERRY *jumps.*

         HARRY *re-enters.*

         Go on.

KERRY   What happened?

HARRY   Nothing just. Dropped a plate. Jo dropped an expensive plate.

KERRY   I should go.

HARRY   No.

KERRY   What am I doing here? Jo doesn't want me here.

HARRY   Jo's fine. It's all fine. She just gets a bit excited. It's all fine. Now, tell me what Bradley did so I can have a quiet word with him and then break the little cunt's neck.

         KERRY *smiles.*

         Come here darling. It's okay. Jo loves having you here.

KERRY   Harry I need to talk to you, I need

         JO *enters with an absurd array of items on two trays.*

JO   Now Kerry I'm not going to let Harry get in the way of you having a chocolate finger.

         I also have a choice of HobNobs, ginger snaps, pink wafers – it's a family box, I can take you through them – plus sugar or sweetener if you are

one of *those*, and a couple of mugs including the
one I think you're gonna go for, '*I'm a Scorpio*'.
Are you a Scorpio Kerry you didn't answer?

KERRY *starts to cry.*

Capricorn.

Have you upset her?

The mobile starts ringing. It's in the kitchen.

THREE

A few minutes later. HARRY *and* KERRY *are eating pink wafers.*

KERRY   Complications?

HARRY   Sounds like it. It's a crucial stage. If she doesn't
          dilate more in the next hour they'll need to talk
          about other options.
          She'll be fine.
          Are *you* fine?

KERRY   Do I look fine?

HARRY   You look upset.

KERRY   Do you blame me?

          JO *wanders back in on the phone.*

          Exciting for Jo.

HARRY   Auntie Jo!

KERRY   Uncle Harry! (*In a child's voice.*) Uncle Harry,
          Uncle Harry!
          Buy me a pony!

          JO *exits again.*

          Have the rest of this.

          KERRY *puts half a biscuit in* HARRY's *mouth.*

          I joined a gym.

HARRY   A gym?

KERRY   Mm-hm

HARRY   You don't need to join a gym

KERRY   It's not about losing weight

HARRY   You don't need to lose weight

KERRY   I – shut up – well, I do, but it wasn't

HARRY   Ridiculous girl

He reaches out to touch her.

Where?

KERRY *moves back.*

He does it again. She moves back.

Where Kerry Cooper?

KERRY   Here! HERE!

She lifts her top up and grabs her hip to demonstrate fat.

JO *enters, watches for a second and then screams in mock-horror.*

KERRY *laughs, trying to find it funny.*

I was just going.

JO/HARRY   No!

JO   *I* was just going!

HARRY   What news?

JO   Don't push yet Dana, don't push, for the love of God!

How's the staff meeting?

HARRY   She's not sure she can talk about it yet

JO   You won't get away with that.

KERRY   What?

JO   It's just.
           Harry really wants to know

HARRY   I don't

JO   He can't cope with suspense.

HARRY   I can.

JO   He can't. He's fucking nosy – the other day I was
            watching him. He didn't know I was watching him
            but I was. He was on the internet and at first he
            was just having a little wank. I stood there and
            watched him through a crack in the door, having a
            little wank at some porn thing or another.

HARRY   (*Kind of laughing.*) Shut up.

JO   Some teenage girl and two guys squirting cum all
            over her face.

HARRY   She's just

JO   He watched the money shot over and over and
            over. It kind of turned me on to watch him. At first
            I even thought he knew I was there but he didn't.

HARRY   Stop it

JO   I realised he didn't because then he started going
            through my emails. Does anyone fancy a glass
            of red?

KERRY   No thank you.

JO   Harry?

            I'm going to have one.

            JO *pours herself a glass of wine.*

            Are you here cos Bradley fucked someone else?

HARRY   Fuck!

KERRY   What? No!

JO   Oh so someone fucked you?

KERRY   No

HARRY   Jesus!

JO   But it has something to do with fucking, at this
            time of night.

HARRY   What does?

JO   The reason she is here.

HARRY   She doesn't need a reason. She's a close friend.

KERRY   It's a little late for spontaneous house calls Harry.

         I think that Bradley may have assaulted me
         tonight. Sexually.

HARRY   Oh my God, *how*?

JO   You see? Nosy.

HARRY   (*To* KERRY.) Are you are you hurt?

JO   Nosy parker.

KERRY   I'm okay

HARRY   I mean, if it's personal then

JO   *If* it's personal?

HARRY   You don't have to talk about it

JO   Obviously it's personal, she's been *sexually
         assaulted*.

HARRY   Have you called

JO   Although of course sometimes it can be very
         impersonal, which is often the most hurtful thing
         about it

KERRY   We'd been arguing.

JO   About what?

KERRY   We'd been arguing.

JO   About Harry?

HARRY   Jo shut the fuck

KERRY   Yes if, about Harry. He's jealous. Jealous of my
         friendship with Harry. He just gets very

JO   Jealous?

KERRY   Territorial.

JO   Like a dog

KERRY   If you like

JO   Or a gibbon

KERRY   Anyway, we'd been arguing. I said he was being
              paranoid, obviously

JO   Obviously

KERRY   It was ridiculous. We've been friends for much
              longer than we went out, et cetera et cetera, his
              girlfriend's a mate, an ex-student even, et cetera
              et cetera.

JO   He wouldn't touch you with a bargepole et cetera
              et cetera

KERRY   (*Laughs*.) et cetera et cetera

HARRY   Jo you're a fucking idiot

KERRY   She was joking dude, it's alright

HARRY   No she's being a horrible fucking idiot

JO   We've established it was a joke.
              What happened next darling, take your time.

KERRY   So he, he calmed down. And we got into bed. He
              was horny. And I, I wasn't. And then. Well then he
              had sex with me.

              He forced himself on me. Basically.

JO   And you tried to stop him?

KERRY   Not physically

JO   But you told him no.

KERRY   He knew

JO   Of course he knew, cos you'd told him.

KERRY   Well he knew because he just knew

JO   Oh, sorry – you didn't tell him?

KERRY   I shouldn't have to *tell* a man not to

JO   Or try to stop him.

KERRY   We've been in a relationship for three years

JO   Yes.

KERRY   We live together. He knows when I'm sad, when I'm on my period, when I'm lying, he knows when I'm guilty, when I'm happy and when I'm horny. Or when I'm not horny. And he knew.

JO   So knowing you're not horny is tantamount to sexual assault?

KERRY   Knowing I don't want sex and doing it to me anyway is, sexual maybe not sexual *assault* but it's sexual something.

JO   It's sexual intercourse.

KERRY   It's a form of rape.

JO   Rape?

KERRY   A form of it, yes.

          JO *looks over at* HARRY. *He doesn't know what to say.*

JO   But you let him

KERRY   I didn't try to stop him.

JO   Why not?

KERRY   He could overpower me if he wanted.

JO   Yeah?

KERRY   Why should I let it get to that?

JO	Why would it get to that?
KERRY	A fight – a physical fight like that would end our relationship
JO	Just say stop?
KERRY	Or an argument, even, an argument about him forcing himself on me
HARRY	And you don't want that
KERRY	No! No of course not. He's my partner.
HARRY	Of course.
JO	He's your – yes but if he's doing something you don't want
KERRY	He knew
JO	Yes but if you didn't want it, if you don't want it, you have to stop him, you can stop him
KERRY	I shouldn't have to
JO	Yes but he didn't rape you.
KERRY	A form I said
JO	He didn't rape you, he didn't a form of rape you, he didn't formally rape you, he didn't rape you.
HARRY	You cannot tell her whether or not she was raped!
JO	If she didn't say anything and didn't physically try to stop him, then he's going to assume
KERRY	He didn't assume
JO	I think it's reasonable for him to assume
KERRY	Assume what?
JO	To assume that you wanted it! You were okay with it happening
KERRY	Okay with it?

JO	For God's sake, this is a relationship! We all, all of us, we all do things in relationships that aren't necessarily what the other person wants
KERRY	Like have sex with them?
JO	Well yes! Yes sometimes. He trusts you to keep communicating, to make it clear
KERRY	It was clear
JO	But you're not an animal! You're not just some lame fish that
HARRY	Lame fish?
JO	Some – yes some lame fish, some lame dumb animal without the capacity to communicate
KERRY	Animals communicate
JO	THIS IS RIDICULOUS
KERRY	Why?
HARRY	Why?
JO	Because – you (*To* HARRY.) don't you start Because you let him think something, you let him go through with it. If Bradley had known, if he'd known how you were feeling, that in your head you were feeling *a form of raped*, he'd. Well I'm sure he would have been mortified. He's a good man. He's a decent guy, yes I wish he'd stop telling everyone how to eat cos he's got a nutrition degree, but he's not a monster. You've demonised him in your head, casting him as the worst kind of person in the world. All because you weren't prepared to say, 'not tonight darling, I don't feel like it'. Honestly, because that's all you had to say, and instead you just lie there thinking 'this is a form of rape. I'm being in some form raped,' when the poor guy was just trying to have make-up sex with

you. It's the most selfish, manipulative, mean-
hearted thing you could possibly do to a person. In
fact it's you who's raped him. It's YOU who raped
Bradley. How does that feel? I just decide that
you've done something, that you are something,
and I just inform you after the event. You're a
fucking rapist Kerry.

KERRY   Harry?

HARRY   I need to speak to Jo.

JO   Nobody needs to speak to Jo

HARRY   I need to speak to Jo

JO   Jo is fine.

KERRY   Harry?

HARRY   Jo is not fine, Jo is getting very worked up.

JO   Jo is a fucking sea of calm

HARRY   And the reason she is getting worked up. The
         reason.

         Let's get you a cab. Can you go to your mum's?

JO   What is the reason Jo is getting very worked up?

KERRY   I guess, but

HARRY   I'll call you a cab darling

JO   What is the reason Jo is getting very worked up
         Harry?

HARRY   Because I do things like that to Jo all the time.

KERRY   Like what?

JO   Yeah like what?

HARRY   I fuck her when I suspect she doesn't, really almost certainly doesn't want it.

JO   That's not true

HARRY   It's alright.

JO   How is it alright? You calling yourself a rapist?

HARRY   By your argument I'm not a rapist

JO   Not a rap– not a rapist, no, but wrong

HARRY   You just said it wasn't wrong

JO   Not wrong, but, what, you

HARRY   You never want to have sex with me any more

JO   I

HARRY   And yet we have sex all the time.

KERRY   I'd be happy with a local cab.

JO   I do want to have sex

HARRY   I know you don't

JO   I just

HARRY   And I do it anyway

JO	I just
HARRY	Shut the fuck up I do it anyway because I want to
JO	No
HARRY	I do it because I want you
JO	No
HARRY	And you know it. You don't let me because you want me. You let me because you pity me
JO	That's / not
HARRY	If that.
JO	No
HARRY	Or you don't want to hurt my feelings or have an uncomfortable conversation, or you don't want us to break up because you're scared of being alone.
JO	That's not
HARRY	It is true. I sicken you
JO	Harry
HARRY	But I sicken you marginally less than being alone.
JO	Harry stop
HARRY	And what is that but rape?
JO	No
HARRY	I've been raping you for years.
JO	Please stop saying that word.
HARRY	I'm sorry
JO	Please.
HARRY	I loathe what I've become with you.
JO	Stop it
HARRY	I can't do this.

KERRY   I can find a cab on the street

HARRY   I'll call you a cab

KERRY   No no

JO   You should take a dodgy one, get yourself proper raped

KERRY   Would you like that?

JO   Put things in perspective

HARRY   Calling one now.

KERRY   Really, I'll go and hail one, it's easier. On everyone.

KERRY leaves hastily, leaving JO and HARRY alone together.

HARRY stops calling the cab.

HARRY   That got rid of her didn't it?

JO   It's very unlikely she'll find one.

HARRY   Yeah.

Quite a rich irony that it's taken a simple visit from our old friend / Kerry to articulate

JO   'Rich irony', you're such a ponce.

HARRY   It's exactly that attitude that meant you were never a first-class student.

You've got a bit of Wotsit on your leg.

JO   Saving it for later.

HARRY   Come here

She lifts up her leg and he licks the Wotsit crumbs off it.

FOUR

An hour later. JO *and* HARRY *sitting drinking wine and watching reality TV.*

JO   This girl's a Machiavellian genius

HARRY   She's a whorey slut.

JO   That's a tautology

HARRY   Is it? Like a jadey Jezebel. A trampy slapper. An easy floozy.

            Of course now I'm deliberately labouring the point which makes / me a –

JO   Commoratio

HARRY   Commoratio is right. Clever little monkey. I taught you well.

JO   I didn't learn that word from you.

HARRY   Who from?

JO   Chambers.

HARRY   Gordon Chambers and his pervy private seminars.

JO   I learnt a *lot* on those rainy Wednesday afternoons.

HARRY   I'm sure you did, sex drive like yours. Penchant for professors. Never presumed I was the only one.

            It's not a tautology anyway it's more of a logical fallacy. Not all sluts are whores but all whores are sluts.

JO   A whore could do that as a job but not be a slut in her private life.

HARRY   She's a professional slut

JO   She could also be a devoted life partner.

HARRY   She's still professionally obliged to be a slut.
            Hence, logical fallacy.

JO   Oh is that conversation over already?

HARRY   Did you book that appointment?

JO   Yep.

HARRY   When is it?

JO   What?

HARRY   When is the appointment?

JO   Next Thursday

HARRY   This Thursday?

JO   Next Thursday as in a week this Thursday, that's
            what next Thursday means

HARRY   You couldn't get one sooner?

JO   It's not urgent.

HARRY   You need to go to it. / You said you needed it.

JO   I am going to go to it.

HARRY   I'm just trying to help out here. / Irregular
            bleeding while you're on the pill is not always

JO   More or less alright without your help I think.

HARRY   What time is it?

JO   What is this?

HARRY   I just want to know at what time you arranged the
            appointment

JO	'The appointment'.
HARRY	What?
JO	You're so serious.
HARRY	It is serious. When is it?
JO	Why do you need to know?
HARRY	So that I can remind you to go to it
JO	I put it in my diary, thank you.
HARRY	What, this diary?

HARRY *grabs her bag and fishes in it for her diary. She chases him.*

JO   Hey, what the fuck, don't you dare go in there – give it back!

HARRY *fends her off and searches in her diary. He stops.*

HARRY   And there we go

JO   I might have forgotten to *literally* write it

HARRY   You never change

JO   I made the appointment, I just forgot to write it down

HARRY   You didn't make the appointment

JO   Fuck you, I did

HARRY   Just admit it.

JO   Fuck off, you're so controlling just, just fuck off out of my fucking life.

HARRY   Just admit it, I want to hear you admit it.

He's walking towards her slowly, she grabs the diary out of his hand.

I want to hear you say, 'Harry I lied to you. I
didn't make the appointment.'

JO   Fuck you

            HARRY *grabs her face so he's squeezing her
            cheeks. He holds her there, tightly.*

HARRY   Say it

JO   Go fuck yourself

HARRY   Say it. Say it or I'll never let go

JO   You're hurting me.

HARRY   I'm a liar. / Say 'I'm a liar'. Say it. Say 'I'm a
            fucking liar'

JO   Please let me go.
            Harry please let me go

HARRY   (*Soft.*) I just want to hear you say the words
            darling, just say 'I'm a liar. And I lie all the time.
            And I lie because I'm a fucking coward.' It's
            alright, just say 'I'm a fucking worthless liar, and I
            don't even know when I'm lying any more. I've
            lost all moorings in the truth and I'm fucking
            lucky to have you Harry because I'm such a
            fucking worthless liar'.
            Say it, and then we can relax.
            Just say 'I'm a liar' for me.
            Just say 'I'm a liar'

            JO *is struggling.*

JO   I'm sorry

HARRY   'I'm a liar'

            'I'm a liar'

JO   I'm sorry

HARRY   I don't want that. 'I'm a liar'

JO   I'm a liar.

         He lets her go.

HARRY   There we are, wasn't so hard.

JO   I'm going to bed

HARRY   Wanna have sex?

JO   Leave me alone

HARRY   I could get little candles, we could have a bath
         with candles like the advert

JO   Fuck off

HARRY   I didn't hurt you.

JO   You did actually

HARRY   No I didn't

JO   You're weird

HARRY   Everyone's *weird*!

JO   Maybe we should.

HARRY   What?

JO   What you said.

HARRY   Fuck?

JO   No. Separate.

HARRY   Hold on

JO   You're not happy

HARRY   *No one*'s *happy!*

JO   Some people are. You said we should have a
         'thinking week' and then you said you *couldn't
         do this*

HARRY   You said you've got stage three melanoma

JO   You said rape.

HARRY   Yeah well, speech is a cracked tin kettle on which we hammer out tunes to make bears dance.

JO   Oh spare me the Ginsberg

HARRY   *Madame Bovary*

JO   Whatever – you said rape.

HARRY   It's not always Beat Generation just cos I taught you Beat Generation

JO   Did you or did you not say rape?

HARRY   I'm saying let's not concentrate on what I *said*, when you know what I *meant*.
Which you do

JO   Do I!

HARRY   Yes

JO   Do I?

HARRY   Can we calm down, can we just calm down for one second.

JO   Totally calm.

HARRY   *Little Book of Calm.*

Little game?

You can win and we can all feel better.

JO   Go to bed. I'll wait up.

HARRY   Got Twister somewhere. I got a blow job last time we played that, didn't I?

JO	Because you won.
HARRY	Because I won? Wow. Wink murder?
JO	Can't play that with / two people you fucking idiot
HARRY	I know you can't play that with two people, I'm not a fucking idiot. Thumb war.
JO	No way.
HARRY	I declare a thumb war
JO	I don't want a thumb war
HARRY	You always want a thumb war

She starts to play thumb war with him.

No. We'll do it properly thank you.

JO/HARRY   One two three four I declare a thumb war.

Bow.
Curtsy.
Kiss.

HARRY	Hey I know what we *should* do.
JO	Split up.
HARRY	No.
JO	British Museum.
HARRY	Yes but not what I meant.

He almost crushes her thumb, but she dodges.

Open relationship.

JO   What?

She's almost knocked off her stride with the thumb war.

HARRY	You heard me.
JO	Don't be ridiculous!

HARRY   You could finally get that hot fuck with Emmanuel
         out of your system.

JO   I don't want to

HARRY   I could stop worrying about not being enough for
         you plus I could reward myself with the odd
         casual dalliance. We'd tell each other about them.
         It could be – romantic.

         She pins him for a second.

JO   One two three four I have won the – ohhh.

         He's pulled his thumb away.

HARRY   Might reinvigorate our sex life.

JO   Are you serious?

         He gives her a look.

         Bullshit.

HARRY   As long as we stay together, it honestly doesn't
         matter to me if you want to fuck around a bit.

JO   And that's what you want?

HARRY   Of course

JO   One two three four / I have won the thumb war.

HARRY   I'm only human.

         You overextended your hand.

JO   Okay.
         Sore loser.

         They resume.

         So you – owww.

HARRY   Oh, man up

JO   You've been thinking about this

HARRY   Yes.

JO   It's your suggestion, not mine.

HARRY   Is it a good one?

JO   Maybe

            They continue to play. HARRY *has begun to touch her between her legs.*

HARRY   *Maybe?* You don't think it's a good idea?

            JO *shrugs and smiles.*

            You'd catch his eye across the bar, and I'd watch you catch his eye and I'd know. You'd be wearing that shitty little T-shirt you wore the night we first fucked. Grubby little student with a filthy look in your eyes. You'd grab the back of his neck, tongue deep into his mouth. And he'd be powerless to escape you. Powerless to resist.

            Your eyes are on fire.

            You're wet.

            It's okay.

JO   Okay.

HARRY   Okay. Excited?

            She smiles. She kisses him passionately. He pushes her away.

            Gotcha.

            Then he grabs her chin.

            I would never.
            Ever.
            Share you with fucking anybody.

FIVE

About 1.30 a.m. HARRY *comes through from the kitchen with a new bottle of red wine.*

HARRY   I'll have one more glass and then I'm calling it a
         night. She's probably trying to sleep anyway. If
         your mum says there's no news then there really is
         no news.
         Have you checked your phone?

JO   Nothing.

HARRY   Well there you go, if there's no news we go to the
         British Museum tomorrow.

JO   You think?

HARRY   Yeah. We can go there and then we can have a
         picnic in the park and then we can go and see
         a movie

JO   Which movie?

HARRY   Whichever movie you like little petal

JO   What, in English?

HARRY   If we absolutely must.

JO   We haven't got any food for the picnic

HARRY   Well, we'll buy some food. We will buy some
         food on the way. We can get nibbly things from
         the deli.

JO   Nibbly is a fucking child's word

HARRY   But you're my hamster

JO   You don't like buffets

HARRY   Well it's not the same as a buffet is it?

JO   Same principle

HARRY   It's not the same – what I don't like about buffets
         is other people. Other people sticking their dirty

fingers into your food. Into the food you're
expected to eat. It makes me feel sick.

JO   I know darling

HARRY   But it's alright if it's you. Your dirty fingers.

JO   I don't have dirty fingers

HARRY   We can soon fix that

JO   Rude

HARRY   What?

*HARRY moves towards her, takes her hand and
puts it on his cock. He gasps.*

What's that?

*She does nothing. He starts to rub her hand gently
on his cock over his trousers. He opens her fingers
to clasp them round him and she doesn't resist.*

JO   Do you want a blowie?

HARRY   Yep

JO doesn't move.

HARRY throws her hand off.

Y'know, every museum I've ever been to on
holiday, in Greece, Egypt, there's always an empty
space with a sign saying 'there used to be
something really cool here but now it's in the
British Museum'. And I've lived in London for a
decade and I've never been.

JO	Harry.
HARRY	It's madness. The whole world's inside and it's right on our doorstep.
JO	Harry I was going to, I just
HARRY	I used to do things. On my own. I used to leave the safety of my home and go and do things.
JO	We'll go tomorrow.
HARRY	I saw my mum the other day.
JO	You didn't tell me
HARRY	Saw her in the whole-food shop
JO	Oh Harry
HARRY	She was on her phone
JO	She okay?
HARRY	I saw her from outside.
JO	Why didn't you tell me?
HARRY	Responding to an advert from Gumtree
JO	So you went and said hello?
HARRY	Well of course I did Joanna. She's my mother.
JO	What did you say?
HARRY	Hi Mum.
JO	Did you have a normal conversation?
HARRY	Not really. She was on the pills.
JO	Which is good
HARRY	Which is good which is good, which is very good. She'd like to meet you.

JO	After all these years
HARRY	After all these years. She even remembered your name.
JO	That's great! I'd love to meet her. When?
HARRY	Dunno, doubt it'll happen. She'll have forgotten next time I speak to her.
JO	Oh.
HARRY	Don't pretend you're disappointed
JO	I am disappointed. Maybe you could remind her, maybe we could meet.
HARRY	You don't want to meet my mum Jo. You don't like playing families. And you're not fucking disappointed about it.

JO	Let's do karaoke.
HARRY	Now?
JO	Yeah. Set up the machine.
HARRY	Are you completely insane, it must be two in the morning
JO	I wanna hear you sing. Set up the machine.
HARRY	I don't want to

JO	How about that blow job?
HARRY	I don't want a blow job now.
JO	But you did.
HARRY	You're tired. We've had a long night.
JO	Don't make it easy on me.
	HARRY *laughs*.
	Then JO *laughs*.

HARRY/JO   *Ooooooh*

HARRY   *Easy* on you.

JO   No

HARRY   Is it such an ordeal?

JO   That was a horrible thing to say.

HARRY   Yep

JO   Really awful.

HARRY   You're despicable

JO   I know. I know I am. I hate myself.

HARRY   I should dump your sorry ass just for that.

JO   You should.

HARRY   I might.

JO   I know you might.

JO *reaches for his cock.*

So you're a rapist now huh?

HARRY   That's what I said.

JO   And Kerry's a rapist.

HARRY   Maybe we two should get together

JO   Maybe you could take turns in raping me.

HARRY   Would you like that?

JO   Maybe.

HARRY   Slut.

JO *laughs a dirty little laugh.*

Maybe what you like and what you need are two
very different things.

JO   Oh yeah?

HARRY	Maybe you need taking in hand.
JO	Oh yeah, like how?
HARRY	Well I don't know.
	Maybe you deserve to suffer
JO	Like what, you gonna beat me?
HARRY	I might.
JO	I'm not scared of you.
HARRY	Not yet.
JO	I could take you on.
HARRY	You wanna try me?
JO	Come on then.
HARRY	Come on then.

JO *gives him a little shove.*

Don't push me, I'll have you.

JO	Well put your money where your mouth is then pussy.

JO *shoves him again, he catches her wrists and holds them.*

HARRY	I'm much stronger than you.
JO	But sadly you are a pussy
HARRY	Is that what you think?
JO	Always have been
HARRY	Pussywhipped
JO	Exactly.

HARRY *lets go of her wrists.*

HARRY	I'm gonna give you the count of five to start running. If and when I catch you we'll see what a fucking pussy I am. Are you ready?

JO	I'm not running.
HARRY	One.
JO	I'm not fucking running.
HARRY	Two.
JO	This is the same trick my dad used on me
HARRY	Three
JO	Except I actually was scared of him
HARRY	Four
JO	I'm not fucking running like a baby
HARRY	Babies can't run four and a half
JO	I'm not running.

HARRY   Fi/ve

JO   AAAAAAGGGHHAHHAHHAHAHAHHH!!!!!!

JO screams and runs. HARRY catches her easily, sweeps her up in the air and then down again. She is giggling, he is trying to turn her over and spank her.

The wrestling gets suddenly quite intense and then JO *screams. She has hit her head.*

Ahhhhhhhhh

HARRY	I'm sorry I'm sorry I'm sorry
JO	Oooowww it's okay
HARRY	I'm sorry I'm sorry I'm sorry
JO	It's okay.
HARRY	Come here
JO	It's okay
HARRY	Come here let me see

JO	Get OFF. Let me just – let me just check, it's alright, I'm alright, I just need to check, don't worry
HARRY	I'm sorry I'm sorry I'm so sorry
JO	It's okay, it wasn't your fault.
HARRY	It was
JO	It was yeah you were too rough.
HARRY	I'm sorry.
JO	I know you are
HARRY	I thought that's what you wanted
JO	To bash my head?
HARRY	I thought you wanted me to be all rough and strong
JO	I did, it was fun
HARRY	But now I've hurt you.
JO	It's okay darling.

JO*'s phone buzzes*.

Eight centimetres

HARRY	Oh my God! It's nearly time. Push Dana, push!
JO	Not yet. Not till ten centimetres.
HARRY	How the fuck do *you* know that?
JO	I don't know. Sympathy pangs?
HARRY	We'll have to stay up now. Have another glass of wine.

HARRY *pours*. JO *raises her glass*.

To Dana!

JO	To Dana. And the birth of your child. And the death of your life.

SIX

Around 3.50 a.m. More wine is being consumed. The karaoke machine has been set up and HARRY *is singing 'The Music of the Night' quite well.*

JO *is punching the air encouragingly at the big notes and singing along to bits of it.*

JO	That was AWESOME
HARRY	Shh
JO	That's the best you've ever done it.
HARRY	Shh, there's someone at the door.
JO	There's no one at the door.

A loud knock.

There's someone at the door.

HARRY	Shh.
JO	We don't have to answer it, no one has the right to disturb us at this time of night. We are civilised people
HARRY	We were being really noisy, it's probably Basement Benny.
JO	Stay quiet and they'll go away.
HARRY	Okay

Another loud knock.

JO	It'll be Basement Benny
HARRY	You wish
JO	Basement Benny loves me
HARRY	Basement Benny wants to bone you
JO	Same thing isn't it?
HARRY	To you it is.

JO	Maybe it's cancer at the door. Come for me. Maybe it's the plague of the white arm spots.
HARRY	Maybe
JO	Maybe it's the boy who gave birth to his twin
HARRY	Maybe it's the taxman come to arrest you.
JO	Maybe it's your ex at the door
HARRY	Maybe it's your ex at the door
JO	Maybe it's the true love of your life at the door
HARRY	Maybe it's how much you used to love me at the door.

Another loud knock.

Well let's see, shall we?

He gets a text.

Yeah it's Kerry.

He goes to answer the door.

SEVEN

Less than a minute later. KERRY *is standing in the room with* HARRY *and* JO.

KERRY	Why do you hate me Jo?
HARRY	What?
JO	What? I don't hate you.
HARRY	Of course she doesn't hate you. Have you been
JO	Of course I don't hate you Kerry.
HARRY	Of course she doesn't hate you, have you been home?
JO	Clearly not.
HARRY	You're freezing.
KERRY	I'm fine. Why do you hate me Jo?
JO	I don't! Am I that awful? God I am, aren't I? I'm awful.
HARRY	Where have you been? Where's Bradley?
KERRY	We spoke on the phone. It's over. He said he knew what he had done.
JO	Your boyfriend's a rapist! That's such a load off.
KERRY	I think you heard my question.

JO	Tea?
HARRY	Yes please.
	JO *leaves*.
KERRY	It's over.

I need to get some clarity. I don't know what's going on. I'm starting to go mad Harry I really

think I'm starting to lose it.
Why would I do this to him? Why would I do this?
Why would I accuse him? WHAT KIND OF
PERSON AM I?

HARRY   Kerry calm down.

KERRY   I don't want to calm down, I don't want to calm
down.

You two are

HARRY   We are what we are.

KERRY   I'm never going to be that, I'm never going to
have that.

HARRY   You wouldn't want it, trust me

KERRY   Maybe I would. Maybe it's all I ever think about.

Maybe you know it's all I ever think about.

Harry.

HARRY   This isn't the time

KERRY   Time for what?

HARRY   We can't do this now

KERRY   I am going insane.
You are making me go insane inside my head.

HARRY   Let's go outside, get you some air.

KERRY   I'm okay

HARRY   Come on.

KERRY   I don't want to get some air Harry.

*JO enters with a bottle of dodgy-looking booze
and some mugs.*

JO   She doesn't want to get some air Harry.
             She wants to stay here.

             HARRY *stares at* JO. *She holds his gaze.*

HARRY   What happened to the tea?

JO   This is tea.

             She pours the wine.

             A clock strikes 4 a.m.

             Dong
             Dong
             Dong
             Dong

             KERRY *accepts a mug.*

KERRY   What must you think of me?
             Don't answer that.

JO   I think you're very brave.

KERRY   You think I'm brave?

JO   I think you're the only one in this room who
             knows what they want.

KERRY   I have no idea what I want

JO   Or at least what you think you want.

KERRY   What I think I

HARRY   Okay

JO   You think you want Harry.

KERRY   I don't want

JO   But that's not what you really want.
              From where you're standing, from stolen
              moments, a drink down the pub. Gentle, clever,
              witty, touchingly anarchic, wise he's wise isn't he,
              those quotes.

KERRY   Listen.

JO   Magical memories from your treasured little
              staffroom fling at uni.

KERRY   No

JO   'Uni'

KERRY   It was hardly a fling Joanna.

JO   If you were to tear off the rosy-tinted spectacles
              for a second. Really look at him. Really *look*.
              He's not funny. He makes jokes, but they're
              not funny.

KERRY   He is to / me

JO   He's not as clever as he pretends to be. His single
              contribution to the world of academia managed
              both to be politically correct and blindly
              misogynistic, without ever saying anything about
              anything that meant anything at all. He parrots out
              the same tired old excerpts over and over, he
              doesn't listen. He's not clear. He makes baby
              faces. He has a disturbingly high sex drive. He
              confuses honesty with decency.

KERRY   He

JO   He's gentle, yes. He's very kind and gentle. Ready
              to run you a hot bath after a long day. Ready to stir
              your coffee when you've just put the sugar in.
              Ready to do for you the thousand and one tiny
              little things in your day you never asked for help
              with and could easily do for yourself.

KERRY   I

JO   And worst of all, you know what Kerry? He's
              boring. I have to play solitaire on my phone
              during conversations just to maintain stimulation
              in vital parts of my brain. He interrupts me
              constantly when I'm trying to work, inexplicably
              narrating his every move, 'just gonna go and
              check on the fish.' 'Oop, 'nother email from
              Graham.' 'Leeet's just see what's on Channel 4 for
              a minute'... DO IT. JUST FUCKING DO IT
              HARRY. DON'T TELL ME ABOUT IT, JUST
              FUCKING DO IT.

KERRY   Right

JO   He whines when he's sick, he cheats when he's
              losing, he kisses like a trout and he weeps when
              he cums.

HARRY   Four more

JO   He dances like a girl, his farts smell of acid, his
              breath smells of cunt and he fucks like a rapist.

              HARRY *bursts out laughing.*

              JO *follows.*

              KERRY *starts to laugh, although unsure why.*

              You see Harry? You see? Why do you stay with
              this girl? Why do you? With this monster? When
              she's standing right here, waiting for you.

KERRY   Me?

JO   (*Whispers.*) She's waiting for you Harry.

KERRY   Jo why are you doing this?

JO   That's what you think though, isn't it? Just say it.
              I'm a monstrous bitch. And you could look after
              him much better, couldn't you?
              That's what you think?
              Don't you?

KERRY   You are a bitch.

JO   Don't you?

KERRY   Don't push me Jo.

JO   Don't you?

KERRY   Maybe I do.

JO   Oh.

HARRY   Kerry I'm very sorry. I think you might have
         fallen victim of one of Jo's little jokes.

KERRY   I'm not stupid.

HARRY   Jo is a horrible person sometimes. I'm afraid I
         think we both are.

KERRY   Oh grow up. I wasn't

HARRY   It went too far. I should have said.

KERRY   You were joking, I was jok–

HARRY   I am sorry. And so is Jo.

JO   I don't even have solitaire on my phone.

HARRY   You do, actually.

JO   I was teasing Harry. I didn't mean for you to

KERRY   You did.

JO   Well yes, I did. And it was very enjoyable but now
      I feel guilty.

HARRY   It's late.

JO   Go back to Bradley. He'll give you a form of
      affection.

KERRY   Harry and I fucked six months after you got
          together.

JO   Ooh.

          JO*'s phone rings. She picks it up.*

          Hi Mum. Yup. Okay. Okay. Okay. Yup. Bye.

          She puts the phone down.

HARRY   C-section?

JO   Who do you like best, me or her?

HARRY   Do we need to go?

KERRY   Is. Dana okay?

HARRY   We should be there.

JO   Come on Harry who d'you like best?

HARRY   You should be there.

JO   I concur, but at present, Mr Pearson, there are
          more pressing issues.
          Answer the question.
          Who do you like best.
          Me or Miss Cooper?

HARRY   Both of you in different ways. You because we
          really get each other. Her because she fancies my
          body. Coat.

JO   Complex.

KERRY   Stop it.

JO   Was it just that one time or a few more?

HARRY   Just the once.

JO   All the way in, or just the tip?

HARRY	All the way in.
JO	Her on top or you on top
HARRY	Actually if I remember correctly we went for sideways with her
KERRY	Both of you. / Stop.
JO	Oh with her leg in the air, I know.
HARRY	Yep.
KERRY	What the fuck?
JO	Should we come to some arrangement, where you can fuck her sideways on the weekends?
KERRY	What?!
HARRY	C'mon, hospital.
JO	No?

Everyone okay?

| KERRY | Is this supposed to be funny? |
| HARRY | It's kind of funny.
And it's kind of sad. |

We need to be with your sister.

| JO | Fuck off! It's a C-section, get your own family, stop being such a fucking Care Bear. |

You okay?

| KERRY | Are you *trying* to humiliate me? Because if you are, if you are, well I understand. But we – we. |

We had *sex*. His *body* was – Yes, it was wrong.
And if you want me to say I'm sorry then I'm
sorry. Yes, it happened. Okay, it was four years
ago but – No, I'm not sorry at all, since we're all
apparently being super-honest about things. But
we do have to do *something* because I can't stop.
Thinking. About Harry. I know – yeah it was four
years ago – I have no claim over him any more,
but he's the closest thing – I've ever felt – Harry,
you know – and there comes a time when a person
has to say. What they want. Just say it out loud
and see if they can get it. And if this is the way
I'm going to get it then so be it.

I love you Harry.

JO   I'm impressed.

KERRY   Fuck you

JO   I'm actually genuinely impressed.

KERRY   I don't understand.
            I don't understand *you* Jo.

            You're

            You're so fucking

JO   Special?

KERRY   Boring.

            You are so. Fucking. Boring.
            Who wants to live like this?

JO   Do you wanna see me cry?

KERRY   Actually, I do. It might help me locate the human
            being.

JO   What can I tell yer?

KERRY   I remember you. You were one of my favourite
              students. One of the first classes I ever took, you
              were in it. I think I was trying to describe the
              concept of being truly 'in the moment'. Do you
              remember that?

JO   I don't think I do.

KERRY   And I was struggling to think of an example, and I
              was a bit nervous, and floundering, so I came out
              with, 'When I'm / making love'

JO   Making love

KERRY   And the boys – this little row of sporty boys. They
              made retching sounds

              KERRY *demonstrates*.

JO   Mm

KERRY   And you told them, do you remember what
              you said?

JO   I don't really remember

KERRY   You said, 'Enough now, little boys'
              And that was it.
              They stopped, because it was you.

JO   Right

KERRY   I never told you how grateful I was for that.

JO   Hey no / problem

KERRY   The first time I ever heard you speak, you were
              kind.

              Is it exhausting?

JO   Yeah.

KERRY   It looks exhausting.

            I'm not the enemy

JO   I know.

            She turns to HARRY.

KERRY   Harry if you can't say what you want now, you'll
            never get it. And you'll never be happy.

HARRY   Jo.

KERRY   What?

HARRY   I want Jo.
            I love Jo.

KERRY   But you don't

HARRY   I do.

KERRY   She won't thank you in the end

HARRY   I don't want her to thank me.

KERRY   You can't make her happy. You can't make yourself
            happy. You know perfectly well what's between us.
            I haven't been alone in this. But now you've forced
            my hand. And so here it is, my hand. I'm holding it
            out to you. Take it. Take a chance, dude!

            JO *mouths the word 'dude' to herself.*

            HARRY *looks at* JO.

            Don't look at her, look at me.

JO   We're a couple.

KERRY   If you're a couple, I'm

JO   The cunt in our living room.

           HARRY *and* JO *laugh*.

KERRY   Why are you laughing?

JO   Look, we got pregnant.

KERRY   I know you did.

JO   'I know you did'

KERRY   You had an abortion

JO   'I know I did'

HARRY   Hey

JO   Oh honey.
           You had an abortion too.

           He's never recovered.

KERRY   Harry wanted that child.

JO   Well, I didn't, so I WIN.

KERRY   Why didn't you want it?

JO   Because I didn't love Harry enough.

           No, I just wanted it to be dead.

KERRY   Well then it's a good thing for that baby that it is.

JO   Sort of wish we'd had it now. Would have been
           cosy.

KERRY   Tell her. Tell her what you told me.

           How when you cut your hand last month you felt
           grateful that all you had to worry about for a
           whole afternoon was losing blood rather than the
           knowledge that your entire life is slowly dripping
           down the shitter? Told her how you fantasise

about squeezing her neck until her eyes pop out
and her tongue folds back and her body twitches
and twitches until it stops twitching altogether.
How she wrecked your reputation, killed your
baby, broke your heart. How she brings out all the
worst of you, how she patronises and demeans
you, how she pushes and pushes and pushes you.

HARRY   How she hurts me.

KERRY   *Yes.* Come with me.

HARRY *looks from* JO *to* KERRY.

JO   Kerry would be kind to you Harry.

HARRY   Kerry can fuck herself.

KERRY   Right.
          Right.

HARRY   You should go.

KERRY   Righto.

HARRY   Kerry.

          I'm

KERRY *leaves*.

HARRY *looks at* JO.

JO   If that was for me you needn't have bothered. I'm
          pissed and I won't remember it in the morning.

          HARRY *tops up her drink*.

EIGHT

About an hour later. HARRY *is standing.* JO *is laughing.*

HARRY   Do you want me now?

JO   No.

          HARRY *is subtly changing his physicality or voice ever so slightly.*

HARRY   Now?

JO   No.

HARRY   Have you checked your phone?

JO   Still nothing.

HARRY   Now?

JO   No.

HARRY   Now?

JO   No.

HARRY   Now?

JO   Sure, yep.

HARRY   You're a fucking treat, you are.

JO   I'm bored of you.

HARRY   Only boring people get bored

JO   That so?

HARRY   That's what my mum used to say.

JO   She must have been bored shitless then.

HARRY   What do you want from me Jo?

JO   I want you to take control.

HARRY	Of what?
JO	Surprise me. Wipe the smile off my face.
HARRY	You want me to hit you?
JO	Do whatever you want
HARRY	For fuck's sake tell me what you want. What do you want?
JO	Rape me
HARRY	Cliché.
JO	Cop-out.
HARRY	You want me to 'rape' you?
JO	Maybe Harry. Something. Show me something fucking new. Because one thing's for sure, I don't want you right now.
HARRY	I'm trying to understand you and I cannot understand you.
JO	I think I'm being fucking clear.
HARRY	You want to play out a rape fantasy
JO	It wouldn't be rape if I want it.
HARRY	You want me to *actually hurt* you?
JO	Maybe.
HARRY	You're weird
JO	*Everyone's* weird
HARRY	I don't like this any more
JO	Pussy

HARRY   Are you trying to leave me?

JO   I don't want to leave you.

HARRY   But if this happens – if that happened, you
could leave me. That's what you want, isn't it?
An excuse.

JO   I'm not that clever.

HARRY   Well I'm not that stupid.
So.

Just to be crystal clear:
Are you asking me to be sexually violent with
you, against your will?

JO   Yes.

HARRY   Don't play with this.

JO   I'm not playing.

HARRY   But if you've agreed then it's not / against
your will.

JO   Oh use your imagination Harry.

HARRY   You want me to do it in a way that would make
you not want it?

JO   Yes

HARRY   You want to be scared?

JO   Yes

HARRY   You want to be hurt?

JO   Yes

HARRY   I don't want to hurt you.

JO   You hurt me all the time.

HARRY   Not physically.

JO   What's the difference?

HARRY   There's a massive difference.

JO   Maybe.

HARRY   You never want to have sex with me anyway.

JO   I want you to act.

HARRY   What if I book you some therapy, is that an act?

JO   Do you know what, forget about it.

HARRY   Okay good.

JO   You don't get it.

HARRY   I don't get it.
              I don't want to get it.

JO   Okay.

              HARRY goes to JO and holds and kisses her.

HARRY   So I dance like a – what, a girl? Is that what
              you said?

JO   A lady.

HARRY   A lady. That I kiss like a trout?
              That my breath smells of cunt?

              *He breathes on her. She tries to wriggle away,
              amused. He doesn't let her.*

              I've got big shoulders. I can take you on. You
              can't push me away.

              He moves on top of her.

              That I fuck like a rapist?

              We've established that isn't true

              I'm good at fucking you.

              He moves his leg between hers.

Women don't ask to be raped.
You don't want to know what it feels like.

HARRY *puts his hands around her throat and starts to grind roughly against her.*

You are such a little bitch. You're nasty. You're manipulative. You're arrogant. You don't know what you want. You want to be dominated but you hate the lack of power. You want to be cleverest but you resent it when you win. You loathe yourself. I'm the only one who understands you.
And that.
Is why.
I will never.
Be.
Alone.

HARRY *undoes* JO's *trousers and pulls them down.*

He kisses her neck and pushes up her shirt.

She doesn't react.

He unbuckles his trousers.

He pushes her hands up above her head and draws her towards him.

Phone beeps. She gives it to him. He stops and reads it.

Risky to push. Reluctant to C-section.

JO   Stuck.

HARRY   They're gonna wait and see.

JO   Maybe it'll never come out.

HARRY   Fffuckit.
            Alright, come on then.

NINE

Around twenty minutes later.

JO   For FUCK'S SAKE HARRY why do you have to
            ruin EVERYTHING / you fucking TOUCH

HARRY   Sorry, sorry, we'll carry on, pretend I didn't / say
            that.

JO   Too late. You've ruined it.

HARRY   You were so fucking convincing. Can I help that?

JO   I told you to keep going. I knew you'd / fuck it up.

HARRY   I told you we should have had a safe word.

JO   Fuck the safe word, we don't need a fucking
            safe word.

HARRY   Let's try again.

JO   No

HARRY   Come on

JO   You were born a pussy and you've remained a
            fucking pussy for your whole sorry life. Pussy.

HARRY   Let's try again

JO   It's no use. You don't understand. You'll never
            understand me at all.

HARRY   I'm gonna rape you again

JO   I told you what I wanted. I couldn't have made it
            more plain.

HARRY   Let's try again

JO   Haven't we emasculated you enough? What do
            you actually want from me Harry? Do you think I
            don't notice your eye-rolling, your cold sweat,
            your fear of anything outside of your dull sexual
            routine? Do you get a kick out of this? Out of all

this humiliation, my humiliation? Do you, you
little yapping. Whippet.

HARRY   Fuck off.

JO   Wow.
That's all you've got.
Let's call it a night.

Do you know what, I'm unreasonable to you.
I shouldn't expect you to understand anything
about women.
I should've taken a leaf out of your mother's book
and left when I had the chance. You bored her out
the door.

HARRY laughs.

He hits her.

A sharp slap across the face. It hurts.

She turns back to him and smiles.

He hits her again, same side.

Hello

HARRY punches JO very hard in the face.

It sends her careering across the room.

She is on the floor.

He watches her, breathless.

She forces herself to look at him.

JO *is torn.*

She looks for a moment as though she will laugh.

He looks like he might laugh with her.

JO *cries.*

The sobs get heavier.

HARRY *goes to her, picks her up and sits her down on the sofa.*

HARRY *strokes her hair.*

HARRY   We are special.
We are above rules.
We are invincible.

Tell me I'm right.

No one understands us better than we understand each other and if we break up, it doesn't matter because we will find our way back to each other. Because I know that in the end, after all this is over, we are truly special and we understand each other in a way no one else ever will.

Tell me I'm right or I won't be able to cope.

She embraces him.

TEN

Around 8 a.m. Sunday. JO *and* HARRY. *There is a bruise on* JO*'s face.*

JO   An. Actual. Baby.

HARRY   You wanna go?

JO   Uh. Not / right now.

HARRY   I understand.

JO   You understand what?

HARRY   You. I do understand you. We'll go when you're ready.

JO   Thank you.

HARRY   It throws stuff up for me too.

JO   I bet.

            HARRY *kisses her.*

HARRY   Let's celebrate. I wanna feed you.

JO   British Museum?

HARRY   Do they sell food? Let's get a picnic.

JO   I want salmon Eggs Benedict. At that café.

HARRY   It's Eggs Royale and anything for you my darling.

JO   Yeah Eggs Royale. I could eat a blue whale

HARRY   I could eat a. Bison and a horse.

JO   I could eat a baby.

HARRY   I could eat you.

JO   I should take a shower.

HARRY   Nah. Fuck it.

JO   Shall we just go out like this?

HARRY   Definitely.

JO   How do I look?

HARRY   Like a Rembrandt.

JO   That's not a huge compliment is it

HARRY   He painted tender pictures of women he loved.
         Bruised, vulnerable women, beautiful as fuck

JO   Alright, come on then.

HARRY   Come on then.

         HARRY *darts out of the room.*

JO   I'm fucking hungry

HARRY   Getting the bag!

JO   Might be pregnant

         HARRY *re-enters.*

HARRY   Bad joke.

JO   I am actually pregnant. Again.

HARRY   In that case we should definitely get you food.

JO   Harry I'm pregnant.

HARRY   Eggs Royale for three then.

JO   I'm being serious.

HARRY   And so am I Joanna! Smoking for three.

JO   Don't

HARRY   Drinking for three.

JO   I'm an idiot.

HARRY   You're a liar.

JO   Four tests. I'm a mummy.

HARRY   You're perverted.

JO   No.

    I'm pregnant.

HARRY   When did you find out?

JO   Last week

HARRY   What about the pill?

JO   I must have forgotten to take it.

HARRY   I saw them in your bag, you've / got them in
    your bag.

JO   I must have not taken it.

HARRY   WHAT THE FUCK IS GOING ON?

JO   Calm down.

HARRY   Did you come off the pill?

JO   Do you want it?

HARRY   I

    Yes.

    Do you?

JO   Yes.

HARRY   Look at me.
           Jesus. You are serious.

           My heart. Is breaking.

           I'm so happy.

           I mean I – When you – when *we*
           Last time
           Every fibre of my being was screaming 'this is
           wrong', and I knew, I knew, I could just *feel* that
           you knew it too.
           I couldn't let myself believe that
           But everything makes sense.

           Irregular bleeding bullshit.

           JO *smiles*.

           You came off the pill you sneaky bitch!

           I love you, you weird, hormonal pregnant woman
           of mine, no wonder you've been so fucking *violent*!

           We are meant to do this. You and me.

           I'm so – WHY ISNT THERE A WORD FOR
           THIS FEELING I'M A FUCKING DOCTOR OF
           ENGLISH!

           I'm happy. I love you. I'm happy.

           You happy?

           JO *nods*.

           No, hold on. Let's not – let's just talk seriously for
           a moment.

           Look at me. Fuck you are beautiful. Okay.

           Question one. Are you willing to do this with me?

JO   Yes.

HARRY   Good. Really good. Question two. Are you willing
            to give up the ciggies and the wine for a little
            while and to be a mother to our child for the rest
            of your life?

JO   Yes.

HARRY   Fuck we are going to be good.
            I will take care of you. We will be brave together.
            Baby steps

JO   Baby steps

HARRY   I love you.

JO   I love you too.

HARRY   What's in your head? What you thinking?

JO   I lied.

            I'm a liar.

            There is no b–

HARRY   No.

JO   Gotcha.

HARRY   Can I kiss you?

            HARRY *kisses* JO.

            Goodbye darling.

JO   Wait, I don't

HARRY   It's okay Jo. You finally found the right words.

            I'll go to a hotel, give you a week to find a place,
            tell me if it's not enough.

JO   You / don't understand

HARRY   I don't blame you. I do understand. You've done
            it. You're.
            Extraordinary.

JO   Harry

HARRY   You're much cleverer than me in a funny way.

            Bye.

            JO faces away from him.

            Bye.

            *HARRY opens the door but then shuts it without
            leaving.*

            HARRY watches JO, she is not aware of him.

            She breathes a huge sigh of relief.

            He continues to watch her.

            End.

A Nick Hern Book

The One first published in Great Britain in 2014 as a paperback original by
Nick Hern Books Limited, The Glasshouse, 49a Goldhawk Road, London W12 8QP,
in association with Soho Theatre

Reprinted with revisions in 2014, 2016

The One copyright © 2014 Vicky Jones

Vicky Jones has asserted her moral right to be identified as the author of this work

Cover image: Michael Windsor-Ungureanu
Cover design: Ned Hoste, 2H

Typeset by Nick Hern Books, London
Printed in Great Britain by Mimeo Ltd, Huntingdon, Cambridgeshire PE29 6XX

A CIP catalogue record for this book is available from the British Library

ISBN 978 1 84842 381 7